HOW TO
TAKE CARE OF YOUR

SPHYNX KITTEN & CAT

BY VINCE STEAD

HOW TO UNDERSTAND AND TAKE CARE OF YOUR SPHYNX KITTEN & CAT

Copyright © 2012 by Vince Stead

ISBN: 978-1478209850

www.VinceStead.com

1. THE CHARACTERISTICS OF A SPHYNX CAT

It was in the year of 1966 that the first Sphynx was born in Canada. However, it became famous only after a pair of them was featured as the sidekick to the villain Dr. Evil in Austin Powers movies. According to Cat Fanciers Association, the Sphynx is the seventh most popular breed of cat.

The Sphynx cat is indeed a special cat that is much different from the normal cats with fur as it has minimal body hair. In fact, based on French breed standards, these cats are part dog, part child, part monkey and part cat as no matter what geneticists say, the breed has personality traits of each animal. However though the cats have an alien appearance, they are complete cats and have the mystic and charm, just like other cats.

It was during the first few mating of the Sphynx cat that breeders realized that the cat's lack of hair is attributed to a recessive gene they have. As it takes two gene copies of the trait to express itself, and if each parent has only a copy of the recessive hairless gene, then the resulting litter will produce about one in four hairless kittens. This thus made it difficult starting a large gene pool.

However, it was found out that this hairless gene was an incomplete dominant over the Devon Rex wavy coat gene. This thus led to the crossing of the Sphynx, American Shorthair and Devon Rex to widen the gene pool and which provided Sphinxes' with and without coats for more than 3 decades across the United States and Europe.

However, the Sphynx looks hairless, its skin or parts of it are covered with a fine and practically imperceptible vestigial covering. This covering gives a chamois feel to the skin texture. However, the heterozygous Sphynx, which have only one copy of the hairless gene, generally has more hair than the homozygous Sphinxes' having two copies of the gene.

Wrinkles are very common in the Sphynx cat, however actually they are no more wrinkled than other cats. The absence of fur on the body just makes the wrinkles more visible and of course, makes the cat feel warm and like suede when you touch him or her.

The absence of body fur will make you think that these cats do not produce any symptoms to those allergic to cats. However, this is not true as though these cats do not shed all over your house, they can still make you squeeze. It is the allergenic protein called Fel d1, which is secreted via, sebaceous and saliva glands, which is produced by Sphinxes' like other cats, that triggers cat allergies.

Even though Sphinxes' have no hair, they do require grooming. They have to be regularly bathed to remove the oily sebaceous secretions on their skin. These secretions are nothing to worry about as they occur in all cats. It is just that the Sphinxes' do not have the necessary hair or fur to absorb them.

However if you do not bathe it, the collection of these oils can lead to skin problems. Instead of bathing, you can also occasionally use a sponge or damp cloth instead of a comb or brush to remove these secretions. Make sure you also clean around the ears every day, as these areas are prone to oil buildup.

The Sphynx has a metabolism any supermodel will vie to have. They can eat anything they want without gaining a pound of weight.

In fact, the average healthy female weighs only 7 to 9 pounds while the males are slightly heavier, at 8 to 10 pounds.

These cats are very loyal and devoted and tend to follow their humans around, while purring affectionately and wagging their tails behind them. They love attention and are just as mischievous and lovable as children are at times. However, not for everyone, the Sphynx cat has an enthusiastic following because of its appearance and charming temperament.

These cats are also very curious to noises, and will do anything to investigate whatever comes into their eyesight. If they are not exploring, you can find the Sphynx on or beside the owner or any other warm object, catching up on beauty rest.

Sphynx cats love entertaining even large audiences. They love attracting attention, love human contact and even play well with other pets. They have high energy levels, which if not channeled, can lead to havoc and mischief. In fact, it is an understatement saying these cats are lively as they are capable of doing monkey like acrobatic feats from doorways and bookshelves.

As the Sphynx has no fur to help regulate their body temperature, they are always looking for some warmth. Though they benefit from the different pet clothing available in stores, they also keep warm with blankets and by curling up with people and pets.

These cats should be kept indoors as they face the highest risk of getting sun burnt. Limit their outdoor time, especially when it is very hot. It is better to apply a cat safe sunscreen on their skin before leaving the house. Moreover, they cannot protect themselves if they end up in fights with other cats outdoors.

Having a cat indoors has its benefit to you, as it is responsible for the death of birds, mammals and lizards coming into your house. In fact, in some countries like Australia, these cats are also responsible for the near extinction of the species.

It is mainly because of selective breeding that these vigorous and healthy cats have few health and genetic problems. However, as the Sphynx digestive system is sensitive, it will give loose and pungent stools if something in its diet upsets their belly. It is always better feeding Sphinxes' raw food as it reduces bowel issues and is a cheaper dietary option than canned cat foods.

The Sphynx is most comfortable with a family that has children. Its high energy and curiosity makes it a great partner for younger children who are always playing and are active. However, this is advised only if the children know how to gently handle the cat.

Even those having other pets make a good home for this fun loving and social Sphynx cat. However as you have to put in lots of time and attention at maintaining the Sphinx's skin, it's better you consider owning a Sphynx cat only if you have prior experience taking care of cats

2. HOW TO POTTY TRAIN YOUR CAT

Did you ever dream that your favorite and adorable precious cat would do his poo in your human toilet and not in the cat litter box? You might have seen this kind of act in the movies and on TV, but you wonder how exactly this could be done. Aren't cats stubborn creatures, with a mind of their own? Can they actually be potty trained? There is a way to do it, but you have to have loads of patience.

The first thing is, if possible, dedicate a toilet, and yes a real toilet for your cat.

The second thing to do is very simple and logical. Just take the cat litter box and place it next to the toilet. Leave it there for a day or so. Let your cat get used to the idea that her litter box and the toilet are close to each other and non-threatening to one another.

Next, raise the level of the litter box from the floor. Do this a little bit at a time by placing thick books like phone books if you have some, to put under it. Do not substitute a box for the books, not yet anyway. This is because a box is naturally taller than a couple of books are. You do not want to create a new and unfamiliar situation. The rise in the height of the box from the floor must be very, very small each time. Do not threaten your cat unnecessarily by changing the box's height abruptly. Do it as gradually as possible. Patience is the best way you are going going to get your cat to do this for you.

As the litter box's height increases, take off a bit of litter from the box. Again, do this gradually. This is because you do not want to create anything unfamiliar to your cat.

After a few days, the height of the box should now be close to the height of the toilet. In addition, if all is right, your cat will do her stuff in her box, as usual. Take care to ensure that the box is secure, because as its height increases, it may fall when your cat jumps onto it, and will mess the whole process up.

Now, move the box nearer to the toilet seat. Gradually that is, until it is about one inch into the toilet seat, and later, directly over the seat. By this time, the amount of litter in the box should be very, very little.

At this point, your cat should already have the idea that she should urinate and defecate in the toilet area. The real transition now begins, where you use a 'training toilet' and keep decreasing the amount of litter in the box.

Specifically built commercial cat potty training devices can help you at this stage of the training. Each comes with instructions, which you must follow closely. You must always pay attention to your cat's safety, because in doing this and if the training toilet is not placed securely, your cat might fall into the toilet bowl.

There will come the 'moment of truth' when you finally remove the training toilet altogether. If you carry out the training well, your cat can figure out what to do next.

The whole process is a slow one, and all the while, you might be wondering if your cat will ever get it. That is a valid concern, but you really do not have much to lose, other than a bit of your time in the weeks that this training is carried out, and it's a cool trick to show your guests!

3. ITEMS YOU SHOULD NEVER LET YOUR CAT EAT

Although cats may seem to be more resilient than dogs, where their digestive processes are concerned they are approximately about the same. A cat reacts much the same to some foods as dogs and often the reaction may be fatal. As with aspirin or valium pills, they can kill your pet very quickly and painfully, so if you think your dog or cat has a headache or they are very agitated the best thing is to take them to a vet and have the problem looked at.

Medications for animals may sound very similar to one you yourself take, but they do not contain all the substances the human drug does and far less of anything pain either relief or antibiotic.

Humans often are on diets, of which tuna is a major food for the human, but it is not the same as the tuna your cat eats, and your cat will suffer malnutrition should you decide to feed her what you yourself are eating. The human tuna does not have the vitamins and minerals that your cat needs to help his and her bones and body remain healthy, and therefore he or she will suffer slow starvation.

We are always told not to feed cat's onions or garlic because of a substance in these, which damages the nervous system. Well, this includes baby food, the little snack that your pet can grab from under the high chair can build up in their system and give your cat problems. Some baby food has onion or garlic salt added to give the food flavor and this will build up in the animal's body and possibly poison it.

You may enjoy a drink of alcohol after work or at a party, but it is not wise to see how drunk your animal can get by deliberately feeding it alcohol. Horses, elephants, and cows can drink some alcohol without too much problems, but because they are so much smaller in body mass than we are as a rule, cats cannot handle it at all, and excrete it very slowly. All the while, their brain and nervous system are receiving irreparable damage as well as other vital organs.

Too much alcohol can kill a cat very painfully, so never let your cat near the alcohol.

Many of us like to bake and the baking powder or soda we use is also not at all good for our cats. Try not to let them lick any of the spilled substance up as it can behave very badly with their electrolytes and other body fluids, such as urine. It can also cause congestive heart failure or severe muscle spasms.

4. How To Trim Your Cat's Nails

The best way to trim your cat's nails is really to start handling its paws when it is a kitten. Gently grasp the paw and massage them until the claw pops out. Work on each separate claw and should your kitten get tired of this, let it go and don't make a big deal about it. Do it gently and your little kitten will soon get used to it, especially if you combine it with petting that the kitten has shown a liking for, such as stroking him or her under the chin.

You can usually teach an older cat to tolerate their claws being played with in the same way, though it may take longer. Adding a little treat if they sit still long enough to do all the claws on one paw is enough usually for one time.

So don't push it otherwise the cat will know something is going to happen and disappear quickly as they are quick to pick up anything odd or strange that is being done or is going to be done to them.

Sit the cat on your lap and turn its face outwards while you play with the paws. Do not exert too much pressure, as the part that the claws is sheathed in is like the finger where the nails is, not covered in much skin at all, and hurts very quickly if you push hard on it. A cat extends its claws very quickly, so it is usually very easy to get them extended if you practice for a bit, without making a big deal about it again.

At no time, allow your children to cut the cat's claws, for they may not see where the quick is and give a nasty painful cut to the claw, ensuring the cat never allows you to go near the claws again. If you can't do it yourself or with the help of another grown up person, then take the cat to a salon that specializes in this type of work, or even to the vet. It is worth the money for the cat will never fully trust you again if you simply scruff it and attack, and you may find your cat even runs away from home, never to be seen again for some reason.

Claws that need trimming are usually long, like fingernails or toenails and may be split or frayed. On dark colored claws, it can be hard to see the quick, where the nail is darker, so simply tip them and cut away the frayed parts, but do not trim the sides of the nail. A very sharp pair of nail scissors can be used, but special scissors can be bought to do this grooming job also.

5. SOME FUN WAYS TO ENTERTAIN YOUR CAT

Cats can amuse themselves quite well without human interference, but sometimes we like to have more interaction with our cat or cats. We just might like our curtains left hanging up and not on the floor with a very upset cat tangled in them. Climbing around on top of a cupboard is also highly entertaining to a cat, as is knocking everything down while it tries to catch a bug or a fly, which was foolish enough to show itself.

If you prefer your cat to use far less energy but still get exercise then use the light of a laser pen to amuse him or her. Moving the light from the laser pen along a wall can give your cat quite a bit of exercise as it tries to catch the light, and the look of absolute concentration they can achieve while catching the beam you will rarely see on any other animal.

An empty toilet roll gives kittens especially good exercise if you can roll it until the cat or kitten grabs and rolls around with it. Cats though, are very insecure about their dignity and it is no surprise to find, if you burst out laughing for too long, to see the cat stalk off with its tail in the air and an expression of ' You are here to entertain me, I am not here to be laughed at' on its face. Kittens are not as easily insulted as will be seen in most games you can play with them.

A ball of wool can involve much catching, throwing and kicking with the back feet. Don't use a ball of wool that you are going to be using later for some knitting though as you will find it very frayed after a few games of this. Proper wool does not take too kindly to this treatment, but the synthetic will to a certain extent. Try not to let the cat or kitten chew off bits of the wool and swallow it either, because it may turn into a hairball.

If your house has a reasonably long hallway in it, then a Ping-Pong ball can provide fun for a while. Some cats will even learn to retrieve the ball, but be prepared for teeth marks, as the difference between a dog's mouth and a cat's is quite large.

A dog can grip a ball without damage, but a cat must hold the ball between its teeth properly in order to carry it, much the same, as it would prey. A Ping-Pong ball is too large to fit in-between a cat's teeth like a dog's, so they must bite it hard in order to carry it. Simply roll the ball along the hallway and allow it to bounce off the walls until your kitten or cat grabs it.

6. HOW TO CLEAN YOUR CATS EARS CORRECTLY

Cat lovers out there are always worried about cleaning their cat's ears without hurting them and in the right way. Regular care is essential for keeping your cat's ears from mite infestations and other such infections. A routine inspection and cleaning can detect any such infections well in advance and can take necessary steps to avoid severe health problems.

Cats' ears normally gets problems such as allergies, bacterial or yeast infections, mite infestations and fungal infections. When practiced on a regular basis, cleaning and inspecting your cat's ears from a very small age, as most cats normally gets used to it without having any issues. The following aspects need to be kept in mind while caring for your cat's ears.

Make the cat feel comfortable when you clean the ears. You can treat your cat to some snacks while you carry on with the ear cleaning. Make sure that the cat is in a happy mood. This means that, you should never try to clean an angry cat's ears or just after a bath, etc...

Handle with good care and make sure that you are holding the cat in a position that is much comfortable for the cat so that the cat doesn't get hurt from being excited.

You can use your forefinger and thumb to roll up the inner skin of your cat's ears, whereby you can clearly see the inner surface of the ears to clean the area. You can also use your remaining fingers to get a good grip on your cat, in order to hold him or her without sliding from you.

Look for any waxy substances and discharges inside the ears. Light brown color wax is normally seen in all kind of cats, which is a good indication as the cat is having natural ear care. However, if the discharge is of dark brown, black, green or yellow in color, it needs attention as it indicates some sort of infection. Pus and such discharges can be wiped away gently with an ear cleaning pad before taking further steps.

You can also drop some five to ten drops of an ear cleansing liquid into your cat's ears and massage the outer base portion of his or her ears for few seconds. A cotton ball can be used to clean the inner surface after the above cleansing is done.

If you see your cat is shaking his or her head more than usual or if he or she seems to scratch their ears frequently, then it might need a veterinarian's attention and further medical care. Make it a routine to inspect your cat's ears along with a regular body checkup. In this way, you can assure your pet a healthy and full life.

7. WHAT YOU SHOULD KNOW ABOUT CAT TEETH

Oral care is one of the most significant parts when it comes to the overall healthcare of your beloved cat. Cats especially are a group of pets that requires extreme personal attention. The cat's mouth in the wild is a lot more different from the ones that are domestic. The former gets its oral care done naturally when it chews on different materials while it catches its preys in the wild etc... Whereas the latter is mostly fed with packed food which even though is much rich in terms of a healthy diet, adds on to poor oral care. Hence, much care needs to be given manually to your lovely domestic cat.

It is always better that the pet owner himself or herself doing a routine oral examination of the pet at home. You can do this by putting one hand at the back of the cat's head, whereby gently stroking the cat you can take a look at the front teeth of the cat by lifting the upper lips with your fingers. You can do this examination at one side first.

This will aid in examining the gums and the other part of the teeth.

If you think that the cat will cooperate, you can try prying the mouth open by slowly pushing its lower jaw down gently. Now, even if your cat doesn't allow you to get a detailed examination, a quick observation while he or she yawns will give you an idea on any overall discoloration or so. Nothing is equal to brushing the cat's teeth on a daily basis, when it comes to cat's oral care.

One important thing to keep in mind while caring for your cat's teeth is that, never try to use human friendly things for a cat, unless it is proven non harmful. Some people tend to use human toothpaste for example for cleaning their cat's teeth, which is in fact never a good idea. There are cat friendly toothpastes available, which are mainly flavored with malt, meat and fish for cat's likeability. The best part of such toothpaste is that they are specially made for cats and hence rinsing is not required and the purpose is met by swallowing the paste. Also, available in the market are cat toothbrushes and oral cleaners, you would be surprised!

Even though the above said is an easy way for cleaning your cat's teeth, nothing is as equal as cleaning it manually with a brush. This might appear tedious, but if you practice with your cat this habit from when it is a kitten, then the matter can be solved easily! If you might have acquired your cat when he or she was full grown, it is better to follow the toothpaste swallowing procedure as otherwise it can even end up in harmful situations for both the cat as well as the owner.

Always remember to feed your cat with specially made foods that are designed to clean up their teeth, do regular checkups and give special attention during any unusual symptoms.

8. How to Make Sure your Cat is Eating a Healthy Amount of Food?

Cats are well known as finicky eaters among all other pets out there. The truth is that, yes, cats are a bit choosy, whatever breed it belongs to. They prefer a proper diet rather than a changing menu. They have a great sense of taste and smell. Most cat lovers get confused on checking out whether their cat is taking a healthy and considerable amount of food on a daily basis. This can be answered if you invest some time in studying the cats' eating habits in detail.

Cats are pets that love to follow a systematic eating habit, which involves a routine diet, feeding time etc. They prefer not to share their food with some other pets (even if it's a cat!). A sudden change in the menu will not be welcomed at all. They would rather prefer a new food item being gradually introduced along with larger portions of their favorite items.

You also need to look into the nutritional requirements of the cat's food sold out there in the market. This is because cats are one set of animals that requires some unusual nutrition. This includes Vitamin A, taurine, niacin and essential fatty acids.

The amount of food and frequency of feeding is of great concern. Kittens, usually less than twelve weeks of age needs to be fed at least 4 times a day. An adult cat can be fed twice a day. You also need to keep in mind things such as, never allow your cat to roam around in a neighboring house, developing a begging behavior by feeding with scrap food etc., all of which can lead the cat to have a bad habit routine.

As with cats, it has been seen that they prefer to consume well and stay healthy when you feed them with meat-based cat's food rather than a vegetable based one. Canned and moist food is also preferred by cats. However, you need to make sure that you're moist and canned foods are never left behind if not eaten. Once opened, the dry foods can be used as a tooth cleaner while kept in a feeding pan for the best part of the day, which also serves as a snack for the cats.

Plenty of clean water is also a necessity with cats as with any other animals. However, make sure that you provide them with clean and non-contaminated water as they are choosy even when it comes to water. If your cat gets around to eating some leaves and grasses, it might be a possible indication of improper diet.

Always make sure that you feed your cat on time with a regular routine. Never hesitate to get a veterinarian's consultation when you suspect any sort of abnormalities with the cat's eating habits. Remember, a healthy cat is the one that follows his or her personal cat's routine.

9. The Different Kinds of Worms Cats can Get

Worms are always a trouble to cat owner, when it comes to taking care of their health. To aid the treatment, it is a necessity to identify the type of worms that your cat has. Here are some worms that cats usually get. There are mainly three types of worms that cats can normally get. They are: Tapeworms, Roundworms and Hookworms.

Out of the three types of worms, the most common culprit is tapeworms.

Tapeworms: Cats usually get tapeworms from eating meat that is uncooked, rodents or even from fleas that are infected.   These worms get into the walls of cat's intestine and passes out its eggs along with the cat's stool.   Worm segments or eggs can be identified from the cat's stool, which usually will be pinkish or whitish in color.   In severe conditions, worms are also seen in cat vomit.   Other symptoms include weight loss, reduced appetite, bony appearance, hair loss etc.   Treatment is available where tablets for deworming are normally prescribed.

Roundworms: Ascarids are the most common type of round worms.   These cylindrical worms are pointed at both ends with white body color.   They are mostly infected via preys such as cockroaches or rodents.   Kittens get ascarids mainly through mother's milk.   Symptoms are almost similar as that of tapeworms.   Kittens are normally seen to possess higher levels of threats in cases of roundworm infestations.   As the ascarid worms are slightly resistant when compared with tapeworms, a regular cleaning of stools and litter pans is advised.

Hookworms: Hookworms are less common in cats, and are found in hot and humid areas. Rotten meat preys and breast-feeding are potential entry points for hookworms. Penetration through the skin is possible for larvae, which later migrate to the small intestine of the cat. Severe diarrhea, anemia, stools that are dark red or black in color, rashes in between the toes etc., are common symptoms.

Usually hookworm infestations of severe cases need your cat to be admitted with the veterinarian for complete cure. In addition, the litter pans and stools need to be cleaned off from time to time with hot water.

If you suspect your cat to be infested with any kind of worms, remember to take a sample of its stool to your vet and get a test done as a preliminary step. Also, follow the vet's advice in getting your dewormer, as some dewormers can be toxic with higher dosages. If you decide to continue on buying such dewormers from a pharmacy, it might not also work on all worms.

You need to be careful with cross contamination issue as well, whereby in a multi cat atmosphere (household) necessary arrangements need to be done to separate and identify separately each cat's stools. Their pans and belongings should also never be interchanged with other cats.

10. How to Deworm your Cat

Owning a pet, especially a cat can be a lot more stressful, if not enough attention and care is given to the animal's health issues. Vaccinations and other treatments are needed from time to time for cats. Along with all such care, deworming them is equally important as well.

Cats, especially the kittens and the old ones are much more prone to worm infestation. Kittens are mostly born with some kind of worm infection, through their mother's milk. Old cats are also easier in being infected through their surroundings. Knowing in detail the type of worms and the deworming methods will aid in approaching a vet for help.

Deworming should be of your prior concerns when it comes to stray cats. Cats that come with a greater linking for preys are of 100% sure, carriers if worms. There are mainly three types of worms that infect cats, tapeworms, roundworms and hookworms.

Tapeworms get into the walls of cat's intestine and passes out its eggs along with the cat's stool. Roundworms are mostly infected via preys such as cockroaches or rodents. Kittens get ascarids mainly through mother's milk. Rotten meat preys and breast-feeding are potential entry points for hookworms.

Tapeworm segments or eggs can be identified from the cat's stool, which usually will be pinkish or whitish in color. In severe conditions, worms are also seen in the cats vomit. Symptoms with roundworms are almost similar as that of tapeworms. Severe diarrhea, anemia, stool that is dark red or black in color, rashes in between the toes etc. are common symptoms when cats are infected with hookworms.

A sample verification of the cat's excreta at the vet is the first step in identifying the infection and furthering the treatment methods. These worms can have longer inactive periods and quick active stages, which might make the identification tedious at times.

Most deworming medications come either as pills or in liquid form. You need to remember that most cats are choosy and have a keen sense of taste and smell and might not properly consume the medicine for deworming. It is advised to follow the disguising technique whereby deworming medications are mixed along with the cat's food while feeding them.

This can be the hardest part for most cat owners when deworming is required. Never give the cats the pills straight away, as chances of them spitting or vomiting it out is pretty good. Deworming needs to be considered as a combined treatment method where, along with oils or liquids, you might also need to conduct other medications due to the insusceptibility of various growth stages of the worm larvae to the medications.

Prevention is better than cure. Hence, make sure that your cats get a proper healthy diet and living conditions for a long and healthy life. If you suspect your cat to be infested with any kind of worms, remember to take a sample of its stool to your vet and get a test done as a preliminary step. Also, follow the vet's advice in getting your dewormer and how to use it properly.

11. WHAT TO EXPECT WHEN YOUR CAT IS PREGNANT

If you are a cat lover and love to see your cat breeding and extending the family, you need to be well aware of the pregnancy period of the cat and what happens during this time period. Even though cat pregnancy is considerably easily recognizable and taken care as compared with many other pets, it needs utmost care and attention during the gestation period and after birth. Cat's being very close to humans, love to get attention, pampering and care during this particular time period of gestation.

As with many other mammals, it is difficult to say whether a cat is pregnant or not during the 1st week of gestation. This is because, she won't be showing much visible symptoms of pregnancy and behavior also will remain the same. In the next few weeks, if you suspect your cat to be pregnant, the first and foremost thing that you need to do is to check her nipples.

You can do this during the normal regular oral checkup, cleaning time or during the health checkup time. After about 3 weeks of gestation, cats will have their nipples turned pink in color. This is a good indication that the cat is pregnant. Mostly this is clearly visible when she is getting pregnant for the 1st time in her life.

After this period it will take almost another 6 weeks our more to deliver her sweet little kittens... i.e. a gestation period of almost 2 month (8weeks). Even though you can clearly identify the pregnancy from such simple symptoms, it is always better to get it confirmed by your vet.

Once they are under the pregnancy period, they become quieter and love to sleep more than usual. Their heat cycles will be suspended for the time being and their interest in male cats will be lost. The domestic cats that used to love walking and roaming outside will tend to spend much of its time back inside home, mostly sleeping as mentioned just a second ago.

Gaining weight is normal during the pregnancy period and visible weight gain is seen usually till the fifth week of gestation. After the 5th week, the nipples will also grow to a considerable size and will be ready to lactate once the kittens are out.

As with their appetite, they will love to eat more during this period and it is pretty good for the mother's health too. You need to feed her with more food, but don't over feed her. Mixing her food with kitten food is good before delivery days. It is also seen that the expecting mother cat drops their appetite at about the 5th week of gestation.

Knowing the cat pregnancy in detail will enable you in taking care of the mother cat and the babies safely, sound and smooth during and after the period of gestation and delivery.

12. TRICKS YOU CAN TEACH YOUR CAT

One doesn't really think much about tricks you can teach a cat. We are prone to think of the family dog as being the one who will do tricks. It is true that dogs tend to be more eager to please. But there are tricks you can teach your cat that are fun to do and fun to show off to friends when they come to visit as well.

Cats are aloof and they have their own opinions about how things should go. But they still respond to rewards and punishments and to affection and praise. Cats are also quite smart and they will learn that certain behaviors get them food or love. Knowing that cats respond to that kind of stimulation gives you all you need to develop a nice collection of tricks you can teach your cat.

One of the easiest ways to develop a nice routine of tricks you can teach your cat is to offer him or her a treat they love so that he or she gets interested in it every single time.

It could be a special commercial cat snack or something as simple as a tiny bit of hot dog or cheese. For example, if you show the treat to your cat and then hide it, he/she will begin to reach out to you to stop you from pulling it away. Repeat this game until he/she "waves" at you and then give her the reward.

Repetition is the key to training any animal so if you repeat this little game, your cat will enjoy playing with you and learn that lifting her paw a certain way will always result in a treat. Before long, all you have to do is lift your fingers like you did when you had the treat and she will "wave" at you on command.

You can use this same technique for lots of tricks you can teach your cat. Repeat the process but instead of teaching her wave, gently touch her paw and "shake" it. Be sure you do not pinch her paw as that will not be accepted as a loving gesture. But that simple shake will become associated with the treat and before long, your can will know how to shake hands.

The trick that we teach dogs to roll over is easy to add to your roster or tricks you can teach your cat. It is not hard to find a time when your cat rolls over naturally.

Cats love to be on their backs and he/she will often do that when you come near in hopes of getting her tummy rubbed. So reward her with that loving rub but before you do so, wave your hand over him or her as a signal that the love is coming to them. If you repeat that motion, they will eventually associate that wave with the tummy rub and roll over for that motion every time.

Using love, play and food, there are many kinds of tricks you can teach a cat. Simply take motions or behaviors that your pet already does naturally and develop them into a trick that he/she will repeat based on a command or a motion and they will perform for you reliably time and time again.

13. WHY CATS LIKE TO CLIMB UP THINGS

Cats are amazingly athletic in their ability to run, jump and climb. When you think about how powerful their legs are as you watch a cat jump many feet into the air, it makes you glad they are so small and that they like you. Any time you bring a new kitten into the home, you will notice how much they love to climb. It can be pretty aggravating watching a kitten climb up the curtains until you get a chance to train the cat not to do that.

It doesn't have to be a big mystery why cats like to climb up things. You may have the temptation to think that they are doing it to be naughty. But keep in mind that even a smart domestic cat is still an animal and that she does not know that climbing is against the rules until she is trained to stop. That is why knowing why cats like to climb up things will make you more patient with your animal.

When your kitten climbs the curtains or the side of the couch, it is usually in the course of play. It is good to recognize, however that to a cat, play is a rehearsal for real events that happen in the life of an animal in the wild. Even though your cute kitten is a house cat, she has all the instincts that came to her from that history of the species as wild animals. That history included hunting and running away.

Cats who live in the wild must hunt to survive. While your cat does not have that problem, that instinct continues in her just the same. Climbing is a skill that nature gives to the feline species to be able to hunt prey for food. All you have to do is watch your cat chase a squirrel or bird in the back yard to see that instinct in full use. This does not mean that when she climbs your curtains or your leg that your cat is hunting for food. That use of climbing in play is part of how cats are wired as well and it is why cats like to climb up things.

Maybe an even more important skill that any wild animal needs to survive is the ability to escape when being hunted by a foe. All you have to do is play chase with your cat so see how good she is at escaping. The skills that nature gives to even house cats to get away include running, leaping, fighting and climbing.

A cat can go up a tree in lightning speed when it is on the run from harm. The problem is that sometimes they cannot get back down.

Understanding that why cats like to climb up things has to do with instinct makes it easier to deal with it when your domestic pet does that. She really is not trying to be bad. It is part of being a cat just as much as purring and cuddling up on your lap. The good news is that with some gentle training, you can teach a cat to keep those climbing skills for outside and to leave your expensive curtains and furniture alone.

14. HOW TO MAKE HOME MADE CAT FOOD

There are a number of good reasons to learn how to make homemade cat food. If you are thinking about going that route, be alert that your veterinarian may discourage it. Keep in mind that most veterinarians sell cat food so they are not interested in seeing the profits of the big pet food companies go down. So take that advice with a grain of salt.

Cost and the health of your cat may be two of the best reasons for learning how to make homemade cat food. It might seem that the fuss and difficulty of creating delicious and healthy food for your cat would be a drawback. However, when you think about how much money you are saving not buying "gourmet" cat food for your pet and that fresh food is so much better for your fluffy friend that the fuss and effort will turn into a labor of love that will actually become a fun cooking project for you each week.

It is good to go into the process of learning how to make homemade cat food with the spirit of adventure. You may need to experiment to come up with the perfect recipes to use to make food for your cat. It pays if you have a good feel for what she already likes to eat. Some cats like fish and others like meat, cheese and various vegetables you may mix into your home made cat food.

After you have a good idea that your cat likes, be sure you educate yourself in how to prepare meals that fulfill all of your pet's nutritional needs. There is very online to help you make sure you are giving your cat good food and plenty of it. You will have a decision to make when sorting out how to make homemade cat food about whether to cook it or to serve the food to your cat raw. As a rule, it is probably smart to cook meat to avoid any chance of salmonella poisoning.

Cooking the meal also makes it easier to turn into edible cat food in your food processor. This is an important step because when you run the food processor with all of the ingredients in your recipe for how to make homemade cat food, you can be sure nutritious things go in that will not be noticed by your animal because of the good things that are in there that she loves.

You can get more information from your pet store or your veterinarian about any supplements to slip into the mixture when you are running your home made cat food through the food processor. It's a good idea to keep a journal of what you cook for your cat so that you can try different recipes to see how she responds. When you have completed your first batch of cat food for your animal, serve it to her in small amounts so that there is not much left in the dish to go bad.

Once you know how to make homemade cat food, you can store each batch in the refrigerator for a few days. That way, you can make up larger amounts and feed it to her over time. However, be careful that you keep your homemade cat food fresh and delicious so that your cat loves mealtime even more with your recipes than she ever did when she ate that store bought cat food out of the can.

15. HOMEMADE CAT TOYS YOU CAN MAKE YOURSELF

You never really have to buy a cat toy for your cat when there are plenty of homemade cat toys you can make yourself. Cats make terrific pets but the one thing that any cat owner will tell you is that their cat has a mind of her own.

Part of the charm of a pet cat is that the animal will have her own ideas about what she wants and that idea is not open to negotiation. Therefore, when you start to think about getting a fun cat toy for your pet, it is good to think about how she likes to play. As you watch, it is natural to ask if your pet would like a cat toy that you might buy or if you could get by with homemade cat toys you can make yourself.

It is great fun to watch a cat play. Cats are amazingly playful creatures and they will play with you or with just about any object, they come across if the cat is in the mood.

In fact, many cats can play with things or creatures that do not seem to be there at all. If anyone ever suggested that a cat does not have an imagination, you know better if you have ever seen your cat play with tremendous energy with something that to human eyes is not there.

If you go to a pet store or even to the pet department of your local Wal-Mart or grocery store, you will find plenty of cat toys you can buy. There is nothing more frustrating than putting a new cat toy you paid for in front of your cat only to see her turn away from it in a huff to go play with a bug.

Realistically, you never have to buy a cat a toy. The number of simple items that you already have around the house can be used with great success to keep your cat entertained for hours. Here is a list of simple homemade cat toys you can make yourself.

A string with a ribbon tied to the end will keep a cat amused for hours.

To encourage your cat to have fun hunting, put a feather under a newspaper with the tip out for her to see. She will stalk it all afternoon.

In addition, empty paper bag will become a fort for your cat. Cats love the rustling sound it makes when they run in and out of it.

Things that move are great fun for cats including an ice cube or a small rubber ball. When she swats it and it escapes, she will think it is alive!

Put a little catnip in a sock you don't need and roll it up and put it in another sock. Watch as your pet pounces on that toy over and over again.

The ideas for homemade cat toys that you can make yourself are endless. There is no reason to buy cat toys when your pet will play with all kinds of inexpensive items you have lying around. In addition, if she can play with you as well as with that toy, so much the better for both of you!

16. WHEN SHOULD YOU SPAY OR NEUTER YOUR CAT?

If you want to know when you should spray or neuter your cat, please read on and learn more. When the ovariohysterectomy of the female species is described, it is called spraying. On the other hand castrating a male species is known as neutering. Both are surgical treatments and can be done by a qualified veterinarian. This makes the cat incapable of having babies in future. The procedure is very beneficial for you and your cat.

When is the right time to spray or neuter? When the cat is as early as 8 weeks old, the procedure can be done easily, by a qualified vet. It is strongly recommended that they get the neutering done early, since it would be healthier for your cat, and the cat population doesn't increase.

Is it important to have your cat neutered? Yes, it is important to have your cat neutered. Take a look at the animal shelters around; there numbers are increasing and the population of cats with them increasing by the day. Would you rather have the current cats neutered and avoid over population or would you want them to grow only to be left out and euthanized later on? Not everyone is a willing adopter, due to many reasons. Some even abandon their pets, again for various reasons, hence neutering your pet helps.

The health and behavioral benefits: When you neuter the cat, he would live a happy life and a longer life, not to forget a healthier life. When you spay, she would be devoid of the mating heat-crying syndrome, when she is in heat. In addition, there is a lot of mess when the cat is in heat, and she would thank you dearly for getting her spayed on time, which avoids such a mess.

When you neuter the male, he wouldn't have sexual desires, there wouldn't be aggressiveness in him, nor would he want to roam wild and aimlessly. When you neuter the males, it would prevent cancer of the testicles and his prostate gland wouldn't enlarge, so the risk of having perianal tumors can be ruled out.

I hope that now you might understand why neutering and spaying the cat would be good for them. Always speak to your vet and then make a decision on whether the pet needs to be neutered or not.

17. WHAT YOU SHOULD KNOW ABOUT FLEAS AND TICKS

Fleas, Ticks, Mites and Lice are some outer parasites that will drive your cat and you both crazy. It will involve your kitten or cat constantly scratching and biting trying to get the fleas and other parasites off them. When you see your kitten or cat using their hind legs to scratch their ears, and using their teeth to try to dig into their skin, it's a pretty good sign they have fleas or a more serious problem.

You can usually get rid of most parasites like fleas and ticks with good quality shampoos and more. One of the things you need to remember is that the eggs that these little parasites leave behind, can take from days to weeks to months to hatch. You need to make sure you kill all the eggs on bedding materials and other places your pet frequents and stays.

Fleas are a common problem for kittens and cats, and they are known to carry and transfer tapeworms sometimes. A good flea spray or shampoo, or other products should work fine. They do have other brands that you usually apply once a month, that usually will take care of the problem the best, and are on the more expensive side, but well worth it.

You should not use any chemicals on pregnant or nursing mothers, as this could harm the puppies or newborn litter.

Ticks are a problem as they can carry Lyme disease and other diseases. Cats usually get these from trees and bushes, as the parasites fall onto the cat's hair, they then attach themselves to the skin, and suck the blood, and sometimes will suck the blood of humans as well.

If you see a tick on your cat and you want to remove it, do not just pull on it. The head might snap off and stay imbedded into your cat's skin. Use pet shop oil for removing ticks, and try to drown and suffocate the tick, and then use tweezers to wiggle the tick back and forth until the whole body becomes free.

If your cat gets lice, you will be able to spot them pretty easily. You would usually need to get a good quality shampoo or insecticide for lice from your local pet store, and it will usually take several applications to make sure they are gone.

If your cat has mites, it is best to take them to the veterinarian for a checkup, and get special medications for your type of mites. There are many different kinds of mites, so your vet should be able to identify them. Left untreated, it will get worse and worse. Some of the mites to look for are around the ears, with dark spots that look like small scabs, but are actually mites eating your dog. Some mites you cannot see unless the vet uses a microscope, and for this reason, you should take your cat in right away if you suspect mites, and to help get rid of your cat's discomfort.

18. What the Benefits of Micro chipping Your Cat Are to You

If you've been wondering if micro chipping your cat is a good thing, it is, if you ask me. It's just like anything, if you ask seven different veterinarian's the same question, you might get some very different answers and opinions, so just use your common sense.

A microchip that is placed inside your cat, usually between the shoulder blades, and with a syringe that looks pretty much like the one cats get their shots with. The microchip is about the size of a grain of rice. It is inserted by your veterinarian, and different vets sell different packages, but relatively all the same.

It is really no more painful to your cat then them being vaccinated. If you ever lose your cat, this is one of the best ways of hoping to get him or her back.

The microchip is basically a transmitter, that the skin just grows right back over, and it stays with your cat, for their entire life. The transmitter does not require any batteries or maintenance. It is embedded with a number the company supplies and your veterinarian will have much more details on, you will have to pay a onetime fee for this service.

When a scanner that a vet or animal shelter should have on hand these days, maybe some smaller out in the country vets still don't have access to one, but if they do, the scanner would make the transmitter give off a signal, that the scanner could read. Since it is universal, injecting the microchip behind the shoulder blades, but over time and years, some cats may have growth movement.

Millions of cats get lost every year. One of the best ways to make sure your kitten or cat does not get lost in the first place, is to be a responsible pet owner. Make sure your home and yard is kitten and cat proof, just like you might do for a real baby in your home.

Make sure fences and gates are secure, make sure there are no holes being dug you don't know about. Make sure your cat gets plenty of exercise and care and love, so they don't feel the need to go elsewhere.

If for some reason your cat becomes lost, the collar and tags might be lost or removed, and then it is nearly impossible to find the rightful owner sometimes, and the worst you can imagine might happen. With the microchip, it is not a for sure bet, but your odds are much higher of getting your lost cat back, then if you did not have it.

Hopefully your kitten or cat has a very nice place to live, either indoors or outdoors, and they like their surroundings, and never dream of running or getting away. But if for some reason, they are in heat, or they hear kids playing, or the mail delivery person coming, and they want to escape, or they just get loose by accident. Like a small child leaving the door open, and then they are long gone, that microchip is going to play a much bigger role in finding him or her, and I really hope it works for everyone!

19. HOW INVISIBLE FENCING TYPICALLY WORKS TO TRAIN AND PROTECT YOUR CAT

Hopefully this will give you a basic understanding on how invisible fencing for your cat should work, and if it is for you, or not for you. Only you can decide if you agree with invisible fencing. Not all yards are the same, and by no means, not all cats are the same, but it should work for most people that use it correctly.

The system would usually entail you trenching a trench, or digging up the ground along the path you want your invisible fencing to go. Just pretend it is an invisible wall, and where you put the wires, will be where the invisible fencing will be located.

You would want to check with your local utilities or power company before digging up and installing the wires. But it is not that difficult for the average person, as long as they follow the instructions carefully for the system they purchase.

Your cat would be fitted with a collar that has some sensors that stick out and contact the cat's skin. From what I hear, the cat does not get a shock, but a surprising jolt, and since cats cannot talk, we will really never know what they feel, until we find a cat that can talk. We can put him or her on television, and they can maybe tell us everything that is wrong with cats and kids would love that story, but you get the idea!

The way it works is you bury the wires underneath the lawn, so you don't have wire everywhere. You can also run it along wooden fences, but not metal ones, and that could be a boundary wall, so they don't dig out, but you don't have to dig up that section, because a fence is already there, basically making them stop digging out, or jumping up on the fence any more.

The collar would require batteries, and a test period, and training sessions with your cat, so that he or she understands what is desired of them. You have to train them properly about where they can, and where they cannot go in the yard. They do have systems for inside the home for cats that jump over gates, and you could find that on the internet for inside places.

You would place red flags along the path of the invisible fencing, for training purposes with your cat. Your cat needs to be able to see the invisible lines first. That is what the flags are put in the ground for. A system that is working fine would give the cat several beeps warning him or her that they are getting too close to the fence.

If they do not move back, they will get a shock or surprise jolt, depending on how you look at it, since the cat can't tell us. The part you really need to teach your cat before you let him or her loose or on their own, is to turn away from the fence, and go back.

You could teach them this by turning it into a fun game for both of you. You would train your cat by taking them up to the fence, and when the warning beeping starts to go off, you could turn around and run, and call your cat to come too! Then when he or she comes, you could give them some praise, and teach them to turn back, not go thru it.

Like anything, you would actually need to teach them to go thru it, so they know what they are in for. Walk with them, and when the warning beeping is going off, let them experience the effect of the surprise.

I'm hoping they are getting a surprise rather than a shock, but if this saves them from running out in the street and getting hit and killed by a car or truck. Or being lose and and lost, then I believe they need to learn what happens if they don't come back, while you are there, rather than while you are away.

You would leave the red flags up until you think your cat is ready for them to be taken down. As with anything you love, take good care of your cat, and watch them and keep an eye on them.

If you just use common sense, and follow the directions on the kit you buy, and don't take any short cuts, do it right the first time, and it will work. Just plan everything ahead of time, and give your cat plenty of time to learn the new system with you, and you both should be happier and safer!

20. WHY DO CATS LOVE CATNIP SO MUCH?

No your kitty isn't on drugs or an addict to stimulants if she is on Catnip. In fact, Catnip also known by the name catnip or even catmint is known to be safe. It is a perennial herb that occurs on a yearly basis and is a member of the family of mints. Any species of the family of cats would love Catnip, be it lynx tigers, mountain lions, lions, tigers or even your kitty at home.

Cats just love to roll over the herb, rub their face in it and sometimes extend their claws or twist their bodies over a bunch of Catnip as well so if you watch kitty at home doing the same, don't panic and rush to the vet, this is normal, for she loves Catnip.

The reason why kitty behaves that way is the strong odor, which is emanated from Catnip there is certain oil in the herb, which has transneptalactone, a chemical in the herb.

The odor of the chemical reminds kitty of a substance, which is found prevalent in any cat's urine. And hence, kitty behaves strange when a bunch of Catnip is offered to her.

Cats go berserk and behave as if they have been drugged when they consume Catnip, but they are actually far away from being intoxicated or drugged. As mentioned, the herb is very safe for kitty and since it belongs to the family of mints, there isn't anything for you to worry about. It is actually the chemical within the herb, which makes the cat behave the way she does when brought in contact with Catnip.

But your home cat may behave very differently to Catnip from what your neighbor's cat may do. Some cats just don't bother all that much about Catnip, they walk away from it as if it is not their botheration, while others go bonkers over it. Those that go gaga over Catnip actually are the ones who find the chemical in the Catnip herb in likely presence to the chemical found in another cat's urine. This chemical actually stimulates the organ of the cat, which makes kitty feel sensations of touch, sight, smells, tastes, sounds etc.

If kitty reacts to Catnip, she would lick or eat it, or else she may just playfully roll and sniff the herb, that's it. Not all cats would respond because the behavior is an inherited feature, just like we humans need to acquire taste for certain foods, the same goes for the feline family as well. If kitty is very young or if Catnip is offered to an old cat, the reaction would be less as compared to those who are young adults, but large cats such as lions would react to Catnip, irrespective of age. Don't bother if kitty doesn't react to Catnip, not all cats do and that's normal.

In conclusion, we can say Catnip isn't addictive. It is like any other treat for kitty, which can be given once a way. The amusing part about this would be the way she behaves once she has Catnip.

21. CAT GRASS

If you have been noticing kitty at home grazing happily on blades of fresh grass, you would have wondered why she does what she does. And this too especially when you serve her the choicest of delicious meals at home. Yet, when she has the chance, kitty would go and chew the grass around like its dessert. However, there isn't anything for you to fret about for her instincts of having a salad or when she pukes it all out.

Actually, the grass juice has folic acid, which is very important for the cat's healthy lifestyle. This is a vitamin, which vets say is available in the mother cat's milk. The vitamin helps the bloodstream of the cat with oxygen production. If there is a deficiency of the vitamin in the kitty, she could suffer in the end with anemia, even her growth would take a beating because of the lack of the vitamin.

It is still a question of debate on how cats know if they lack folic acid in them or not, even the experts cannot answer that. Folic acid supplements are found in abundant by cats when they roam out of home, which they may or may not get naturally when you serve them their meals at home.

Cats cannot tell you, but vets say that the chewing of grass helps them with bowel movements as well. In fact, grass helps as a laxative; it provides fiber and de-worms the cats as well. Even fur and other bulky substances from their intestines are removed with the help of grass. Broad-leafed grass helps with bowels and thin leafed grass helps the cat vomit. Not all said and done, vets still give a clean chit to cats chewing on grass as necessary.

They say healthy cats can manage process matter within without any external help, and it is only the sick ones that would chew on grass. Then there are vets who believe just as humans would pop in an antacid after a meal, the cats chew grass to keep their stomachs settled. And then there is a school of thought, which opines cats love the taste and texture of grass so they chew it.

But after a short while of chewing away on grass, the cat pukes it out. This is because their internals aren't designed with enzymes to enable digestion of grass, and not because cats are non-vegetarians. Through the process of regurgitation, cats also cough out the fur balls inside their system, thus it is a healthy practice for them to chew grass and then puke say experts. This wouldn't allow the cat to feel uncomfortable and you shouldn't punish kitty for bringing it out.

You may find it really awkward that kitty chews grass, but honestly she loves it and she is benefiting from it, say experts. She wouldn't ever eat large quantities of it and if she does so on a daily basis, she could be telling you that she needs a vet to check her. If kitty is a cat that isn't outdoors very frequent, you may want to keep an eye on her grass grazing habits and inform your vet for the same.

22. CAT URINE

No matter how much you try house breaking your cat, he would pee where he wants, period. And the consequences God forbid would be for you to bear. Having said that, pee of a cat can be smelly, no wonder one of the popular characters on a comedy sitcom sang SMELLY CAT!!

Cats are very meticulous about everything they do, including peeing. If they don't have a sparkling (according to their standards) watering hole, they would go find another place to do their business. So no matter how many times you tell the cat "This is your place to pee", consider it being told to the birds and the bees, get the drift.

Now cat pee can smell especially if the cat pee is of a male cat that sprays anywhere he wishes to. They are habitual creatures and no matter how many scolding rituals you may have out him through, he will go search for a spot new and clean to do his business. A spot, which doesn't smell of his urine, that is! So the only way to go about getting rid of the odor is to instantly clean it with cleaners that get rid of the smell on the spot.

What you could do is blot as much as urine possible with the help of paper towels or an old rag. Then take water (3parts) and vinegar (1part) and place it on the pee spot, for saturation. Do the same thing once again to completely dry the place and when it is dry use a little baking soda to clean up the place. After this take ¾ of hydrogen peroxide (3%) solution and a teaspoon of detergent and mix it with the baking soda. Rub it on the pee spot and with the help of an old brushwork in the baking soda mix. When this spot dries up completely, use a vacuum over it and the odor will be gone.

Sometimes cats pee over clothes kept in the laundry, and this would include your bedding, clothing, rugs etc. All you need to do is use one fourth of apple cider vinegar along with a detergent in the washer.

If the cat pees on walls or the floors, instantly wash the area with a cleaner. Then wipe with water to remove all traces of the residue of cleaners. Repeat the step again, and then use a little bleach. The next step would then be to use a bottle spray and use 10:1 water to bleach mix. The area which needs to be cleaned should be well ventilated and don't forget to use rubber gloves when you clean. Spray the area and wait for a minute and then wipe dry with an old rag, the pee smell is gone.

23. THE DIFFERENT BETWEEN CAT SPRAYING AND URINATING

There is always a confusion to know where the cat is urinating or spraying, especially when it's a male cat and he does it not in his litter box but outside. In both cases, the situation isn't too pleasant for you to deal with. However, when you know the difference between the two, it could bring down the miseries associated with it.

Most cats when trained from the time they are kittens would use the litter box, however they would still mark and spray places for territorial reasons and that too every day. They would mark by spraying for many reasons, one of which is for them to attract a mate for themselves. The second reason being to mark their territory, while the other reasons to tell the other cats "back off" from their homes.

If a cat is stressed, spraying could happen, and some cats spray just to ensure effective communication is achieved with other feline members of the community. Cat spraying is not only a form of urinating, what they actually give out is a mix of glandular secretions and urine. In this, you would find many pheromones, which attracts other animals through their sense of smell.

You should look for signs to know if the cat is spraying or urinating. When a cat is spraying, it would stand tall with its tail in the air and its bottom held high. But when it urinates to would crouch and squat, with its bottom held towards the floor. There is also a particular smell for spraying that is different from urination. Experts say the best way to stop the cat from spraying would be to get it neutered. And if you think it is stress that is making the cat do this, find out why the cat is stressed, look for signs.

You should keep an eye on the posture of the cat to know if it is urinating or spraying. Cats can be territorial and thus would use spraying as their method to communicate the same.

This would help them tell other cats about the boundaries and lines they conform to for social standing. Such is the non-verbal communication that it goes without rasps and calls, say experts when cats urinate it helps them release pressure from their bladder, so check the posture as described above and you would know if the cat is spraying or urinating.

The best thing to now do is keep an eye on your cat's behavior and follow what we described for you to know if your cat is spraying or urinating. Once again, if you are confused it would be best to observe your neighbor's cat or speak to a vet who would be able to explain it to you better. Spraying and urinating are natural for cats, especially male cats. Spraying can destroy items around over a period of time, so ensure you learn how to avoid that ahead.

Made in the USA
Lexington, KY
12 March 2014